SIERRA CAMPFIRE YARNS

TALES, SK S

WRITTEN & COLLECTED BY
DEEP RIVER JIM

YOSEMITE
ASSOCIATION

Yosemite National Park, California

Campfires are magic and memories. As words flicker around it, imaginations are brightened. We travel back to distant times, spending the evening as our ancestors did—sharing the day's events, recounting myths and legends, and joking with one another.

Just as a fire burns, campfire programs should start with a lively and spirited blaze. The group is united by boisterous participation in stories and songs. As the fire settles into peaceful flickering flame, quieter taletelling follows. Finally, when the coals begin to glow, the evening winds down with a calming narrative or song. The spirit of the fire carries over in sweet (not scary) dreams for the sleepy-eyed young campers.

A couple of simple suggestions make for a good campfire. One person should be named "keeper of the flame." That individual builds and lights the fire and may add a log or two in the early part of the evening, stirring occasionally between stories. But remember, the fire should burn down as the evening progresses.

A flashlight or lantern—placed behind the readers so they can see the text easily—will prove helpful. It should be passed with the book to a new reader.

Squeegee Hunt is a wonderful participation tale and I strongly encourage giving it a try, even if you've never heard it before.

Special Note
The middle two pages of this book contain the lyrics to some group songs. These pages can be carefully removed from the book ahead of time, cut in half, and handed around.

Yosemite Association
Copyright © 1999

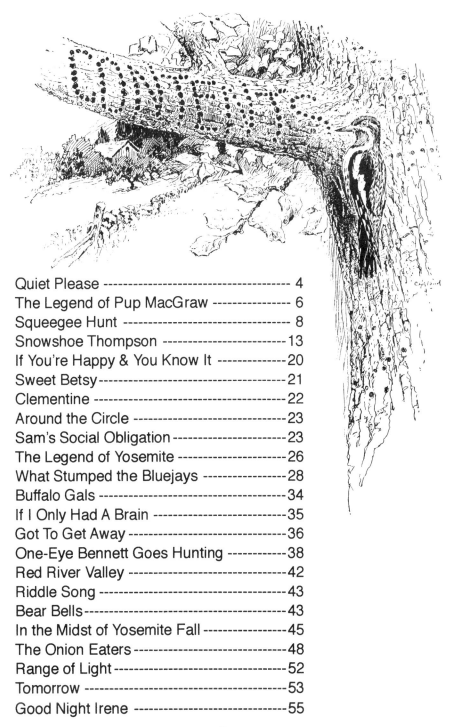

QUIET, PLEASE

The Parts: Assign at least one to each person. When the name of their part is read, they make the appropriate noise.

THREE CHILDREN (sing: Row, Row, Row Your Boat)
THE POLICEMAN (Loud Whistle)
THE FIRE SIREN, TRUCK or DEPARTMENT (Siren Sound)
THE LIBRARIAN (SSSSh!)
THE DOG (Arf, Arf)
THE PIGS (Snort, Oink)
THE DUCKS (Quack-Quack)
THE CHICKENS (Bok-Bok-Bok)
WHEN I SAY "CRASH," Everyone Clap
WHEN I PUT BOTH HANDS UP IN THE AIR, Everyone Scream as Loudly as Possible

Spring had come to the sleepy little town of Markleeville. In the balmy afternoon air the fragrance of early wildflowers mingled with the smell of the nearby pine forest. A hint of skunk cabbage drifted up from the boggy meadows.

Sounds were few. In the distance, the faint moan of the volunteer brigade's **FIRE SIREN** _____ came from a neighboring village. Far off, a **DOG** _____ was barking and periodically an occasional whistle from the **POLICEMAN** _____ directing traffic at the main intersection was heard.

At the town library someone turned a page too loudly and the **LIBRARIAN** _____. On the main road, at the edge of the town, Ernie Silva, a crusty mountain farmer, was driving his animals to market. He was sleepy from the warmth and intoxicated by the springtime smells. Each time he hit a bump, all the **PIGS** _____, every **CHICKEN** _____, and all the **DUCKS** _____. Yes, it was peaceful in the little burg.

Suddenly, **THREE CHILDREN** _____ appeared on the quiet street. They were singing "ROW YOUR BOAT" and were leapfrogging over one another. They reached the center of town where the **POLICEMAN** _____ let them cross the street.

The **CHILDREN** _____, marched up the steps of the library. The **LIBRARIAN** _____ looked up quickly. Each took out a comic book from their back pocket, then sat down at a table. One of them looked around the almost empty library and said, "They'd do a lot more business in here if it weren't for all these books!" Guess what the **LIBRARIAN** _____ said?

Outside, the **DOG** _____ grew louder. The **POLICEMAN** _____ as a car approached the intersection, followed by the farmer's truck. As they started up again, the woman driving the car signaled a left turn. Farmer Silva was half-asleep. He slammed on his breaks, but it was too late. There was a **LOUD CRASH** _____(everyone clap their hands together).

Down went the tail gate of the truck and out tumbled the **PIGS** _____, the crates burst and away flew the **CHICKENS** _____ and the **DUCKS** _____. The **DOG** _____, who by now was quite close, began an excited chase. Frightened, the **PIGS** _____ ran up the library steps, followed by the **CHICKENS** _____, **DUCKS** _____ and the **DOG** _____. The **LIBRARIAN** _____ was so startled she had time to let out only one "SSSSh," before a CHICKEN _____ flew into her face. The **CHILDREN** _____ jumped up and delightedly burst into song. In rushed the **POLICEMAN** _____. From across the street, old Miss Spindle saw the disturbance, and called the **FIRE DEPARTMENT** _____.

5

At that moment in the quiet library of the quiet town of Markleeville, these things were going on: The **PIGS** _____, the **CHICKENS** _____, the **DUCKS** _____, the **CHILDREN** _____, the **FIRE SIREN** _____, the **POLICEMAN** _____ and the **LIBRARIAN** _____ hopelessly. And for awhile at least, all these things were going on at the same time.

But an hour later, everything was peaceful again in the sleepy little town of Markleeville. The **PIGS** _____, **DUCKS** _____, and **CHICKENS** _____ had somehow been caught and put back in the truck; the **CHILDREN** _____ and the **DOG** _____ had gone home for supper, the **FIRE TRUCK** _____ was back in the station house, and the **POLICEMAN** _____ again stood at his post by the intersection.

And the **LIBRARIAN** _____? Well, she looked around the library at the floating feathers, the muddy floor, the mixed up books, the overturned tables and the broken chairs. And then, all of a sudden, the **LIBRARIAN (HANDS UP & EVERYBODY) SCREAMED**_____.

 ## The Legend of Pup MacGraw

Quite a few years ago, a young dog named Pup MacGraw walked into a Carson City saloon. This was well before the town had been modernized – back when folks rode horses down Main Street and the pace of life was of the old and wild West. It was a hot and dusty day.

"Gimmee a beer," said the dog.

Now this was a pretty unusual thing, even for those parts, and the bartender took a long look at the Pup and answered, "I'm sorry, we don't serve dogs here."

MacGraw reached in his vest pocket, pulled out a

$20 gold piece and slapped it hard on the bar. "I said I want a beer."

Things had taken a turn toward the ugly. The bartender, getting red in the face and hot under the collar, said, "I'll tell you once more, we do not serve dogs here. Now git."

Pup growled at him and the bartender pulled out a gun and shot him right square in the foot. The dog let out a high pitched yelp and ran out under the swinging doors.

The next day, at high noon, those same doors were pushed open and in walked Pup McGraw. He was dressed entirely in black – a black two gallon hat, a black scarf around his neck, a black vest, three black cowboy boots and a black bandage on his front foot.

The room fell silent – the piano stopped playing, the gamblers, drinkers and good-time gals stood frozen in place, waiting to see what would happen. Pup's gaze slowly took in everyone in the establishment. He waited a second in silence then snarled, "I'm looking for the man who shot my paw."

Squeegee Hunt

This is a great crowd pleaser and a wonderful participation ditty. One person leads, delivering the lines in a singsong voice — conducting the response from the audience. The

group keeps a rhythm by alternately slapping the top of each thigh. Motions — hand slapping, tree climbing, grass parting, etc. — can accompany the story where indicated.

The narrator should practice once or twice with an assistant beforehand. The motions and timing are easy to learn. Use different rhythms and voice when chanting the lines.

The assistant can also sit next to you at the campfire, keeping a finger pointed to the right place in the text.

Prelude

Only in the remotest canyons, deep in the wildwood of the mountains, lives the elusive Sierra Long-Toed, Ring-Necked, Black-Eyed Squeegee.

The Squeegee spends almost its entire existence far inside caves, emerging briefly each night to eat and drink. Only a handful of the bravest of campers and explorers, risking life and limb, have managed to glimpse this creature. The Sierran Squeegee has never been photographed.

Conditions are right. If you are feeling especially courageous, we can go on a Squeegee hunt right now.

Goin' on a Squeegee hunt,   – *start slapping thighs* –
   (response) Goin' on a Squeegee hunt
Gonna' catch a big one   – *slap thighs* –
   (response) Gonna' catch a big one
I'm not afraid   – *slap thighs* –
   (response) I'm not afraid
What do I need? – *scratch head* –
   (response) What do I need?
Gotta get my trapnet – *slap thighs* –
   (response)
Take it from the tent   – *slap thighs* –
   (response)
Carry it on my shoulder – *slap thighs* –
   (response)
Phew! I'm not afraid   – *slap thighs* –
   (response)

-– repeat chorus – (Goin' on a Squeegee Hunt...)

Gonna' leave the campsite   – *slap thighs* –
   (response)
Headin' up the trail – *slap thighs* –
   (response)
Phew! I'm not afraid – *slap thighs* –
   (response)
What's that up ahead? – *slap thighs* –
   (response)

—repeat chorus—(Goin' on a Squeegee Hunt...)

Look, there's a meadow   *—slap thighs—*
  (response)
Gotta go through it   *—rub palms to make sound—*
  (response)
Phew! I'm not afraid   *—wiping brow—*
  (response)
What's that up ahead?   *—slap thighs—*
  (response)

—repeat chorus—(Goin' on a Squeegee Hunt...)

Whoa, there's a river   *—slap thighs—*
  (response)
Gotta' swim across it   *—swimming strokes—*
  (response)
Phew! I'm not afraid   *—wipe brow—*
  (response)
What's that up ahead?   *—slap thighs—*
  (response)

—repeat chorus—(Goin' on a Squeegee Hunt...)

Ooo, there's a tree   *—slap thighs—*
  (response)
Gotta go climb it   *—hand over hand—*
  (response)
Phew! I'm not afraid   *—wipe brow—*
  (response)
What's that up ahead?   *—slap thighs—*
  (response)

—repeat chorus—(Goin' on a Squeegee Hunt...)

I see a cave   *—slap thighs—*
  (response)
A big, dark cave   *—slap thighs & shiver—*
  (response)
Squeegee's cave!!   *—slap thighs & bigger shiver—*
  (response)

Phew! I'm not afraid   —*wipe brow*—
  (response)

—repeat chorus—(Goin' on a Squeegee Hunt...)

Go to the cave??   —*slap thighs and nod head yes*—
  (response)
Gotta' climb down   —*hand over hand, descending*—
  (response)
Walk to the cave   —*slap thighs*—
  (response)
Phew! I'm not afraid   —*wipe brow*—
  (response)

—repeat chorus—(Goin' on a Squeegee Hunt...)

Here is the cave   —*slap thighs*—
  (response)
Gotta go inside   —*slap thighs*—
  (response)
It's dark in there!   —*slap thighs, crane forward*—
  (response)
I'M AAFFRRAIDD!!!   —*slap thighs slowly, tremble*—
  (response)

IN SHAKY VOICE—repeat chorus—(Goin' on a ....)

What's that up ahead   —*jolt upright*—
  (response)
Boy, does that smell!   —*hold nose*—
  (response)
Yipes, it's furry   —*feel ahead with hands*—
  (response)
Yeow, it's big   —*reaching up, still feeling*—
  (response)
2 big eyes   —*hold up two fingers*—
  (response)
1 huge mouth   —*pry open mouth*—
  (response)
sharp sharp teeth   —*count teeth*—
  (response)

stinky, stinky breath   *—slam mouth shut—*
  (response)
2 wet noses?   *—feel for 2 noses—*
  (response)
SSQQUUEEEEGGEEEE!!!   *—scream it loudly—*
  (response)

———fast———
I'M AAFFRRAIDD!!!
  (response)
It's too dark!   *—start slapping thighs—*
  (response)
Gotta get outside!   *—slap thighs—*
  (response)
Get to the tree!   *—slap thighs—*
  (response)
Climb up the tree!   *—hand over hand, ascending—*
  (response)
Climb down the tree!   *—hand over hand, descending—*
  (response)
Get to the river!   *—slap thighs—*
  (response)
Gotta swim across!   *—swim strokes—*
  (response)
Get to the meadow!   *—slap thighs—*
  (response)
Gotta go through it!   *—parting grass—*
  (response)
Get to the trail!   *—slap thighs—*
  (response)
Gotta head up it!   *—slap thighs—*
  (response)
Get to the campsite!   *—slap thighs—*
  (response)

Gotta get inside!   —slap thighs—
  (response)
Hang up the net!   —throw off shoulder—
  (response)
Hop into bed!   —pretend to be sleeping—
  (response)
— — —**slowly**— — —
Phew! I'm not afraid!!!   —wipe brow—
  (response)

SNOWSHOE THOMPSON

The most remarkable and fearless of all our West Coast mountaineers was John A. (popularly known as "Snowshoe") Thompson. For over twenty years, before rail, telegraph or vehicle, he braved the winter storms, crossing the high Sierra to keep California connected with the rest of the country. His name became synonymous with endurance and daring everywhere in the mountains.

Thompson was a man of splendid physique, standing six feet in his stockings and weighing some 180 pounds. He was quite handsome, with the blonde hair and beard, fair skin and blue eyes of his Scandinavian ancestors. He looked a true descendant of the sea-roving Norseman of old.

In the year 1837, at ten years of age, Thompson left his native Norway and came to the United States with his father and family.

In 1851, Mr. Thompson, then twenty four years of

age, was smitten with the "gold fever," and came across the plains to California.

He landed at Hangtown, now known as Placerville, and for a time mined at Coon Hollow and Kelsey's Diggings. He soon became dissatisfied with the life and luck of a miner and tried his hand at ranching. He lived in the Sacramento Valley in 1854-55, but his eyes were constantly drawn to the mountains, where the snowy peaks glittered against the deep blue sky. He did not feel at home in the valleys; he did not like mining; and for a time he was undecided in what direction to turn.

Early in the winter of 1856, Thompson read of the trouble experienced in getting the mails across the snowy summit of the Sierra Nevada Mountains. This set him to thinking of his childhood in Norway, where ski-like snowshoes were as familiar as are ordinary shoes to the children of other lands. He determined to make a pair of snowshoes out of the oak timber he was engaged in splitting. They were ponderous affairs, ten feet in length, four inches in width and weighing about 25 pounds apiece.

Having completed his snowshoes to the best of his knowledge, Thompson set out for Placerville to try them out. Placerville was not only his old mining camp but was also the principal mountain town on the Old Emigrant Road—the road over which the mail was then carried. The weight mattered little, their owner was a man of giant strength and he was too eager to see if his idea worked to lose time in making another pair out of lighter wood.

Stealing away to secluded places near the town, Thompson spent several days trying his snowshoes. He soon became expert and when he made his first public appearance, he astonished all who saw him.

14

His were the first Norwegian snowshoes ever seen in California—before then the only snowshoes were those of the Canadian pattern. They looked like thin sled runners, and with his long balance pole in his hands, he dashed down the sides of the mountains at a fearful rate of speed.

Snowshoe Thompson did not ride astride his guide pole, nor trail it by his side in the snow, as is the practice of other snowshoers when descending a steep mountain. He held it horizontally before him, after the manner of a tightrope walker. His appearance was most graceful

when seen darting down the face of a steep mountain, swaying his long balance pole now to this side and now to that.

Having satisfied himself with his abilities on snowshoes, Thompson felt he was ready to transport the mails across the mountains. The first trip was made in January, 1856, from Placerville to Carson Valley, a distance of ninety miles. With the mail bags strapped on his back, he glided over fields of snow that were in places thirty to fifty feet in depth, his long Norwegian shoes bearing him safely and swiftly over the surface of the great drifts.

Having successfully made the transit, Snowshoe Thompson proved his necessity and was soon a fixed institution of the mountains. He carried the mails between the two points all that winter, the only land communication between the Atlantic states and California. No matter how wild the storms that raged in the mountains he never failed to get through, generally on time.

15

The weight of the bags he carried was usually from sixty to eighty pounds; but his loads often weighed over one hundred pounds.

From Placerville to Carson Valley, because of the great amount of uphill traveling, three days were consumed. He was able to return to Carson Valley from Placerville in two days, making forty-five miles a day. Between the two points all was wilderness.

When traveling in the mountains, Snowshoe Thompson never carried blankets nor did he even wear an overcoat. The weight and bulk of such articles would have hampered his progress. Exercise kept him warm while traveling and when he camped he always built a fire. He carried as little as possible besides the bags containing the mail.

All he required for food was a small quantity of jerked beef and a few biscuits. He never carried provisions that required cooking. Everything could be eaten as he ran. When thirsty he caught up a handful of snow or drank the water of some brook or spring.

Snowshoe never stopped for storms. He always set out on the day appointed, without regard to the weather, and traveled by night as well as day. He pursued no regular path—in a trackless waste of snow there was no path to follow—but kept to a general route. By day he was guided by the trees and rocks and by night looked to the stars as a mariner to his compass.

Snowshoe's night camps—whenever the evening was such as prevented him from pursuing his journey or when it was necessary for him to obtain sleep—were generally made wherever he happened to be at the moment. He always tried, however, to find a dead pine at which to make his camp. After setting fire to the dry stump, he collected a quantity of fir or spruce boughs, with which he constructed a sort of rude couch or platform on the snow. Stretched upon his bed of boughs, with his feet to the fire and his head resting upon one of Uncle Sam's mail bags, he slept as soundly as if occupying the best bed ever made, though perhaps beneath his couch was thirty feet of snow.

Although Snowshoe Thompson carried no guns when in the mountains, he always carried matches. He kept them safely stowed away in a tight tin can box or securely wrapped in a piece of oiled silk.

"One night," he relates, "I lost my matches in a creek at which I stopped to drink. That night I lay out on the snow without fire. It was very uncomfortable and I did not sleep much, but I had no fear of freezing. When awakened by the cold, I got up, exercised a little, and after that took another nap. So I put in the night."

Occasionally, his slumbers were interrupted by startling accidents. Sometimes his fire, burning downward toward the roots of the stump beside which he was camped, melted the snow underneath his platform of boughs and he suddenly found himself sliding down into a deep pit—a pit filled with fire.

Snowshoe Thompson accepted hardship and danger as an everyday occurrence. He found a great many lost men and saved them from death's door. He was chased by Piute Indians, when they were warring with the whites in Nevada. He never saw a grizzly bear, but often came across their tracks. He was frightened but once, when he came upon six big timber wolves digging out the carcass of some animal. "They looked to have hair on them a foot long. They were great, gaunt, shaggy fellows." As he came close, they sat on their haunches. When Thompson neared, the leader threw back his head and uttered a loud and prolonged howl. All the others of the pack did the same. He showed a bold front and they let him pass.

Thompson was the most expert snowshoe runner in the Sierra Nevada Mountains. By 1870 there were many snowshoers, but in daring Thompson surpassed them all. Near the town of Silver Mountain, in Alpine County, was a big mountain. Ordinary snowshoers would go partway up the mountain to where there was a bench, and then glide down a beaten path. This was too tame for Thompson.

He would make a circuit of over a mile and appear on the top of the mountain. He would give one of his wild high-Sierra whoops, poise his balance pole, and dart down the face of the mountain at lightning speed, leaping all the terraces from top to bottom, and gliding far out on the level before halting. Reports say he regularly made clear jumps of 50 and 60 feet and once, on a mountain in back of Genoa, made a jump of 180 feet without a break.

For 20 winters Snowshoe Thompson carried the mails across the Sierra Nevada Mountains, at times when they could have been transported in no other way. For 20 years he delivered the U.S. mail without a contract for the service. On both sides of the mountains he was told that an appropriation would be made and all would come out right with him, but he got nothing except promises.

To ordinary men there is something terrible in the wild winter storms that often sweep through the Sierra; but the louder the howlings of the gale rose, the higher rose the courage of Snowshoe Thompson.

Yet for such a man there was no real recklessness in anything he did. He watched every mood of the elements and guarded against all danger that threatened. His way was pointed out by every star in the heavens— by every tree, rock and hill—was whispered by the breeze and shouted by the gale. All else might be lost in the wild tumult of a winter storm, but Snowshoe Thompson stood unmoved amid the commotion; there, as everywhere, at home.

And he is still at home, for he rests where the snowy peaks of his beloved mountains look down upon his last camping place; where the voices of the pines are borne to him by every breeze, and where the trembling ground often tells of the fall of the avalanche. A most fitting resting place for such a man.

—Based on a report by **Dan De Quille**

If You're Happy & You Know It

C   G
If you're happy & you know it, clap your hands

                           C
If you're happy & you know it, clap your hands

        F   C
If you're happy & you know it, let everybody show it

       G   C
If you're happy & you know it, clap your hands

2—stamp your feet   3—slap your knees
4—do a dance   5—shout hurrah
6—Shout hurrah, do a dance, slap your knees, stamp your feet, if you're happy and you know it, clap your hands.

Sweet Betsy

C   G   C
Did you ever hear tell of Sweet Betsy from Pike,
                          A minor   D   G
Who crossed the wide mountains with her lover Ike,
    C   F   C
With two yoke of cattle and one spotted hog,
                               G   C
A tall Shangai rooster and an old yellow dog.

They swam the wide river and climbed the tall peaks
And camped on the prairies for weeks upon weeks,
Starvation and illness, hard work and slaughter,
They reached California in spite of high water.

They passed the Sierra through mountains of snow,
'Til old California was sighted below.
Sweet Betsy she hollered, and Ike gave a cheer,
Saying, "Betsy, my darlin', I'm a made millioneer."

Long Ike and Sweet Betsy became husband and wife,
Built up a family and had a grand life.
And Betsy, well satisfied, said with a smile,
"I've got all I need within half a mile."

Clementine

D
In a cavern, in a canyon, excavating for a mine **A7**

D   **A7**   **D**
Lived a miner, '49-er, & his daughter Clementine

O my darling, O my darling, O my darling Clementine
You are lost and gone forever, dreadful sorry, Clementine

Light she was and like a fairy and her shoes were number 9
Herring boxes without topses, sandals were for Clementine
——Chorus——
Drove the ducklings to the water every morning just at nine
Stubbed her toe against a splinter, fell into the foaming brine
——Chorus——
Ruby lips above the water, blowing bubbles soft and fine
But alas! I was no swimmer, so I lost my Clementine
——Chorus——
In a churchyard near the canyon where the myrtle does
    entwine
There grow roses, other posies, fertilized by Clementine
——Chorus——
Then the miner, '49-er, soon began to peak & pine
Thought he oughter join his daughter, now he's with his
    Clementine
——Chorus——
In my dreams she still does haunt me, robed in garments
    soaked with brine
Tho' in life I used to hug her, now she's dead, I draw the line
——Chorus——
O ye campers, heed this warning to this tragic tale of mine
CPR, it would have saved her, oh my darling Clementine

—Around the Campfire Circle—

Everyone tells the favorite thing they did today.

Sam's Social Obligations

Deep in the fastness of the West Walker range, in a steep canyon carved by a tributary of a wild mountain river, lived an old and crotchety hunter, Seldom Seen Sam. If the weather was passable, Sam spent his time in the water, panning for gold or catching monster trout by reaching slowly under submerged logs and overhanging banks, grabbing them with his bare hands. In the winter he holed up in his cabin when the worst of the blizzards hit, otherwise he poked about the mountains looking for the dens of Sierran grizzly bears.

Sam was the independent sort. He lived in a log cabin he had built over the entrance of a cave. In the summer if it got too hot, he would retreat back into the cool inner recesses during the heat of the day. Sam was warm blooded, anything over 55 degrees qualified as too hot for him to tolerate.

Of course, he pretty much always wore a thick pair of woolen underwear, elkskin pants, a couple of deerskin shirts and a long tunic made of the hide of a mountain bear.

23

All this was topped off by a raccoon-skin hat, head and tail intact, which he hadn't taken off for 8 years.

Sam wasn't much of a swimmer, in fact he wasn't much of a bather either. He ate, slept and worked in this outfit and it was a rare time when he'd remove any article of clothing. He figured the dirt and grime that had built up kept mosquito bites from penetrating. Those few who got downwind of Sam guessed a snake bite wouldn't get through either.

Though not much of a cook he managed to survive through the year on wild plants, fish, bear meat, and massive quantities of heavy, leaden doughnuts he deep fried every morning in the grease saved from grizzlies.

Sam didn't do well in towns and cities. His visits to the outside world occurred once in the Fall and once in the Spring—when he'd trade some of his gold nuggets for his necessaries—generally a clean and fresh pair of long undies, powder and bullets for his rifle, and hundreds of pounds of flour to make his sinkhole dough-nuts. He would get so much flour that he'd have to employ a man and mules to pack it back to his claim.

It was because of this that folks found out how Sam would combat the aching loneliness of his lofty mountain retreat. My great-great-uncle, Dewey Tellum, was given a four ounce nugget to haul the flour one spring. Because Sam ate about 5 pounds of doughnuts a day and wasn't going to town again for 6 months, Dewey had to deliver 12 big sacks of Prentiss's Best Blue Ribbon

24

flour. It took a half dozen mules to carry the load.

Following a map Sam drew on deerskin, he led the mules up and up, deep into the Sierra, until he crossed the Sawtooth Ridge and descended into the mouth of the narrow, high-walled canyon Sam had indicated.

It was getting late in the day and Dewey wanted to make it to the upper part of the canyon where Sam lived, but the mules grew tired and finally refused to go further. Uncle D left them grazing in a patch of tender grass along the river and walked around the first bend, only to come on Sam and his camp.

Now Sam wasn't much of a talker and he simply nodded hello to Uncle Dewey. The place was beautiful— steep granite walls on each side of the canyon and the river running through it, splashed with green meadows and wildflowers and groves of trees.

As it grew dark, they sat around a campfire much like this one, and consumed a meal made mostly of Sam's doughnuts. By questioning Seldom Seen Sam, Uncle Dewey was able to find out that the chasm ran north for miles—with high vertical precipices, ending upstream in a box canyon—a canyon that ends with steep cliffs on three sides.

Sam said he never got entirely lonely and didn't have much use for the company of folks, but allowed he did need to hear a human voice now and then just to keep from going crazy. In fact, he said he heard enough jabberin' for the evening and it was time to turn in.

As Uncle Dewey crawled into his bedroll, he saw Sam climb up a small pine near the dying campfire, cup his hands and yell, "Good morning, Seldom" up towards the box end of the canyon. Exactly 8 hours later, to the minute, Seldom Seen Sam woke up, his listening done for the day, as he heard last night's echo booming back into camp, — *"**Good morning, Seldom.**"*

The Legend of
Half Dome

Long ago, Tis-se'-yak and her husband Nangas dwelt in the dry, barren plains, a brown land without trees or water. They heard about the beautiful Valley of Ah-wah'-nee, where waterfalls cascaded into a green fertile valley, and decided to make the long journey there. The path to Ah-wah'-nee was difficult, leading the couple over the high mountains, and Tis-se'-yak carried a heavy burden basket on her back. Nangas followed closely behind her, carrying his bow, arrows and a rude staff.

Tis-se'-yak arrived first in the Valley of Ah-wah'-nee and stopped at the lake called A-wai'-a. She was so hot and thirsty from her long journey that she drank every drop of water in the lake. When her husband reached the lake and found it dry, he became so angry he struck her with his staff and beat her soundly. Tis-se'-yak fled from her husband but he caught up to her and beat her some more. She became enraged at his treatment of her and shouted and flung her basket at Nangas.

As they stood facing each other in fury, they were turned to stone for their bad behavior, and remain there to this day. Nangas stands next to the basket Tis-se'-yak threw (Basket Dome) and Tis-se'-yak's sad rock face (Half Dome) is stained with the dark lines of her tears.

What Stumped the Bluejays

Animals talk to each other, of course. There can be no question about that; but I suppose there are very few people who can understand them. I never knew but one man who could. I knew he could, however, because he told me so himself.

He was a middle-aged, simple-hearted miner who had lived in a lonely corner of California among the woods and mountains a good many years and had studied the ways of his only neighbors, the beasts and the birds, until he believed he could accurately translate any remark which they made.

This was Jim Baker. According to Jim Baker, some animals have only a limited education, and use only very simple words; whereas, certain other animals have a large vocabulary, a fine command of language and a ready and fluent delivery; consequently these latter talk a great deal; they like it; they are conscious of their talent and they enjoy "showing off."

Baker said that after long and careful observation, he had come to the conclusion that the bluejays were the best talkers he had found among the birds and beasts.

Said he: There's more to a bluejay than any other creature. He has got more moods, and more different kinds of feelings than other creatures; and, mind you, whatever a bluejay feels, he can put into language. Why you never see a bluejay get stuck for a word. No man ever did. They just boil out of him!

If I Only Had a Brain

I could while away the hours, conferin' with the
    flowers
Consultin' with the rain
And my head, I'd be scratchin' while my thoughts
    were busy hatching—If I only had a brain
I'd unravel ever riddle for any individdle
In trouble or in pain
With the thoughts I'd be thinkin', I could be
    another Lincoln—If I only had a brain
I would not be just a nuffin, my head all full of
    stuffin'
My heart all full of pain
And perhaps I'd deserve you & be even worthy
    erv you—If I only had a brain

When a man's an empty kettle, he should be
    upon his mettle
And yet I'm torn apart
Just because I'm presumin' that I could be
    kinda human—If I only had a heart
I'd be tender, I'd be gentle, & awful sentimental
Regarding love & art
I'd be friends with the sparrows & the boy that
    shoots the arrows—If I only had a heart
Just to register emotion, Jealousy, Devotion
And really feel the part
I would stay young & chipper & I'd lock it with a
    zipper—If I only had a heart

Life is sad believe me missy, when you're born
    to be a sissy—Without the vim & verve
But I could change my habits, never more be
    scared of rabbits—If I only had the nerve
I'm afraid there's no denyin' I'm just a
    dandelion—A fate I don't deserve
But I could show my prowess, be a lion, not a
    mowess—If I only had the nerve
I would show the dinosaurus, who's big around
    the forres'—A king they better serve
Why with my regal beezer I could be another
    Caesar—If I only had the nerve

Red River Valley

From this valley they say you are going,
We will miss your bright eyes & sweet smile
For they say you are taking the sunshine
Which has brightened our pathway a while.

Come and sit by my side if you love me,
Do not hasten to bid me adieu

But remember the Red River Valley
And the one who has loved you so true.

Won't you think of the valley you're leaving,
Oh how lonely, how sad it will be?
Just think of the fond heart you are breaking
And the grief you are causing to me.

As you go to your home by the ocean,
May you never forget those sweet hours
That we spent in the Red River Valley
And the love we exchanged 'mid the flowers.

Riddle Song

I gave my love a cherry that had no stone,
I gave my love a chicken that had no bone,
I gave my love a story that had no end,
I gave my love a baby with no cryin'.

How can there be a cherry that has no stone?
How can there be a chicken that has no bone?
How can there be a story that had no end?
How can there be a baby with no cryin'?

A cherry as it's bloomin' it has no stone,
A chicken when an egg it has no bone,
A story of "I love you" it has no end,
A baby when it's sleepin' has no cryin'.

Goodnight Irene

**(Chorus): Irene goodnight, Irene goodnight
Goodnight Irene, goodnight Irene, I'll see you
    in my dreams**

Sometimes I live in the country, sometimes I live
    in town,
Sometimes I have a great notion, to get out and
    wander around.   **—chorus—**
I love Irene, God knows I do, I'll love her 'til the
    seas run dry
And if Irene turns her back to me, I'll roam the
    mountains high.   **—chorus—**

Foxes sleep in the forest, lions sleep in their dens
Goats sleep on the mountainside & piggies sleep
    in pens.   **—chorus—**
Whales sleep in the ocean, zebras sleep on land,
Hippos sleep by the riverside & camels sleep on
    sand.   **—chorus—**
Coyote sleeps in the canyon, a birdie sleeps in a
    tree,
And when it's time for me to rest, my tent's the
    place for me.   **—chorus—**

If You're Happy & You Know It

If you're happy & you know it clap your hands
If you're happy & you know it clap your hands
If you're happy & you know it, let everybody
   show it
If you're happy & you know it, clap your hands

2— stamp your feet   3—slap your knees   4—
do a dance   5— shout hurrah   6— shout hurrah,
do a dance, slap you knees, stamp your feet, if
you're happy and you know it, clap your hands

Sweet Betsy

Did you ever hear tell of Sweet Betsy from Pike,
Who crossed the wide mountains with her lover
   Ike,
With two yoke of cattle and one spotted hog,
A tall Shangai rooster and an old yellow dog.

They swam the wide river and climbed the tall
   peaks
And camped on the prairies for weeks upon
   weeks,
Starvation and illness, hard work and slaughter,
They reached California in spite of high-water.

They passed the Sierras through mountains of
   snow,
'Til old California was sighted below.
Sweet Betsy she hollered, and Ike gave a cheer,
Saying, "Betsy, my darlin', I'm a made millioneer."

Long Ike and Sweet Betsy became husband and
   wife,
Built up a family and had a grand life.
And Betsy, well satisfied, said with a smile,
"I've got all I need within half a mile."

Clementine

In a cavern, in a canyon, excavating for a mine
Lived a miner, '49-er, & his daughter Clementine

**(Chorus): Oh my darling, Oh my darling, Oh
   my darling, Clementine**
**You are lost and gone forever, dreadful
   sorry, Clementine**

Light she was & like a fairy & her shoes were
   number 9
Herring boxes without topses, sandals were for
   Clementine   —chorus—

She drove the ducklings to the water every
   morning just at nine
Stubbed her toe against a splinter, fell into the
   foaming brine   —chorus—
Ruby lips above the water, blowing bubbles
   soft and fine
But alas! I was no swimmer, so I lost my
   Clementine   —chorus—
In a churchyard near the canyon where the
   myrtle does entwine
There grow roses, other posies, fertilized by
   Clementine   —chorus—
Then the miner, '49-er, soon began to peak &
   pine
Thought he oughter join his daughter, now he
   with his Clementine   —chorus—
In my dreams she still does haunt me, robed
   in garments soaked with brine
Tho' in life I used to hug her, now she's dead,
   draw the line   —chorus—
Oh ye campers, heed this warning to this tragi
   tale of mine
CPR, it would have saved her, Oh my darling
   Clementine   —chorus—

Buffalo Gals

Buffalo gals won't you—come out tonight,
   come out tonight, come out tonight
Buffalo gals won't you come out tonight &
   dance by the light of the moon

As I was walking—*down the street (3x)*
A pretty girl I chanced to meet beneath the
   silver moon

I asked her if she'd—*stop & talk (3x)*
Her feet covered up the whole sidewalk, she
   was fair to view

I asked her if she'd—*be my wife (3x)*
Then I'd be happy all my life if she'd marry me

Oh I danced with the dolly with a hole in her
   stocking
And her feet kept a-rocking & her knees kept
   a-knocking
Oh I danced with the dolly with a hole in her
   stocking
And we danced by the light of the moon

SONG SHEET—REMOVE AND CUT

If I Only Had a Brain

I could while away the hours, conferin' with the
    flowers
Consultin' with the rain
And my head, I'd be scratchin' while my thoughts
    were busy hatching—If I only had a brain
I'd unravel ever riddle for any individdle
In trouble or in pain
With the thoughts I'd be thinkin', I could be
    another Lincoln—If I only had a brain
I would not be just a nuffin, my head all full of
    stuffin'
My heart all full of pain
And perhaps I'd deserve you & be even worthy
    erv you—If I only had a brain

When a man's an empty kettle, he should be
    upon his mettle
And yet I'm torn apart
Just because I'm presumin' that I could be
    kinda human—If I only had a heart
I'd be tender, I'd be gentle, & awful sentimental
Regarding love & art
I'd be friends with the sparrows & the boy that
    shoots the arrows—If I only had a heart
Just to register emotion, Jealousy, Devotion
And really feel the part
I would stay young & chipper & I'd lock it with a
    zipper—If I only had a heart

Life is sad believe me missy, when you're born
    to be a sissy—Without the vim & verve
But I could change my habits, never more be
    scared of rabbits—If I only had the nerve
I'm afraid there's no denyin' I'm just a
    dandelion—A fate I don't deserve
But I could show my prowess, be a lion, not a
    mowess—If I only had the nerve
I would show the dinosaurus, who's big around
    the forres'—A king they better serve
Why with my regal beezer I could be another
    Caesar—If I only had the nerve

Red River Valley

From this valley they say you are going,
We will miss your bright eyes & sweet smile
For they say you are taking the sunshine
Which has brightened our pathway a while.

Come and sit by my side if you love me,
Do not hasten to bid me adieu

But remember the Red River Valley
And the one who has loved you so true.

Won't you think of the valley you're leaving,
Oh how lonely, how sad it will be?
Just think of the fond heart you are breaking
And the grief you are causing to me.

As you go to your home by the ocean,
May you never forget those sweet hours
That we spent in the Red River Valley
And the love we exchanged 'mid the flowers.

Riddle Song

I gave my love a cherry that had no stone,
I gave my love a chicken that had no bone,
I gave my love a story that had no end,
I gave my love a baby with no cryin'.

How can there be a cherry that has no stone?
How can there be a chicken that has no bone?
How can there be a story that had no end?
How can there be a baby with no cryin'?

A cherry as it's bloomin' it has no stone,
A chicken when an egg it has no bone,
A story of "I love you" it has no end,
A baby when it's sleepin' has no cryin'.

Goodnight Irene
(Chorus): Irene goodnight, Irene goodnight
Goodnight Irene, goodnight Irene, I'll see you
    in my dreams

Sometimes I live in the country, sometimes I live
    in town,
Sometimes I have a great notion, to get out and
    wander around.   —chorus—
I love Irene, God knows I do, I'll love her 'til the
    seas run dry
And if Irene turns her back to me, I'll roam the
    mountains high.   —chorus—

Foxes sleep in the forest, lions sleep in their dens
Goats sleep on the mountainside & piggies sleep
    in pens.   —chorus—
Whales sleep in the ocean, zebras sleep on land,
Hippos sleep by the riverside & camels sleep on
    sand.   —chorus—
Coyote sleeps in the canyon, a birdie sleeps in a
    tree,
And when it's time for me to rest, my tent's the
    place for me.   —chorus—

If You're Happy & You Know It

If you're happy & you know it clap your hands
If you're happy & you know it clap your hands
If you're happy & you know it, let everybody
show it
If you're happy & you know it, clap your hands

2— stamp your feet 3—slap your knees 4—
do a dance 5— shout hurrah 6— shout hurrah,
do a dance, slap you knees, stamp your feet, if
you're happy and you know it, clap your hands

Sweet Betsy

Did you ever hear tell of Sweet Betsy from Pike,
Who crossed the wide mountains with her lover
Ike,
With two yoke of cattle and one spotted hog,
A tall Shangai rooster and an old yellow dog.

They swam the wide river and climbed the tall
peaks
And camped on the prairies for weeks upon
weeks,
Starvation and illness, hard work and slaughter,
They reached California in spite of high-water.

They passed the Sierras through mountains of
snow,
'Til old California was sighted below.
Sweet Betsy she hollered, and Ike gave a cheer,
Saying, "Betsy, my darlin', I'm a made millioneer."

Long Ike and Sweet Betsy became husband and
wife,
Built up a family and had a grand life.
And Betsy, well satisfied, said with a smile,
"I've got all I need within half a mile."

Clementine

In a cavern, in a canyon, excavating for a mine
Lived a miner, '49-er, & his daughter Clementine

**(Chorus): Oh my darling, Oh my darling, Oh
my darling, Clementine
You are lost and gone forever, dreadful
sorry, Clementine**

Light she was & like a fairy & her shoes were
number 9
Herring boxes without topses, sandals were for
Clementine   —chorus—

She drove the ducklings to the water every
morning just at nine
Stubbed her toe against a splinter, fell into the
foaming brine   —chorus—
Ruby lips above the water, blowing bubbles
soft and fine
But alas! I was no swimmer, so I lost my
Clementine   —chorus—
In a churchyard near the canyon where the
myrtle does entwine
There grow roses, other posies, fertilized by
Clementine   —chorus—
Then the miner, '49-er, soon began to peak &
pine
Thought he oughter join his daughter, now he
with his Clementine   —chorus—
In my dreams she still does haunt me, robed
in garments soaked with brine
Tho' in life I used to hug her, now she's dead,
draw the line   —chorus—
Oh ye campers, heed this warning to this tragi
tale of mine
CPR, it would have saved her, Oh my darling
Clementine   —chorus—

Buffalo Gals

Buffalo gals won't you—come out tonight,
come out tonight, come out tonight
Buffalo gals won't you come out tonight &
dance by the light of the moon

As I was walking—*down the street (3x)*
A pretty girl I chanced to meet beneath the
silver moon

I asked her if she'd—*stop & talk (3x)*
Her feet covered up the whole sidewalk, she
was fair to view

I asked her if she'd—*be my wife (3x)*
Then I'd be happy all my life if she'd marry me

Oh I danced with the dolly with a hole in her
stocking
And her feet kept a-rocking & her knees kept
a-knocking
Oh I danced with the dolly with a hole in her
stocking
And we danced by the light of the moon

If I Only Had a Brain

could while away the hours, conferin' with the
    flowers
Consultin' with the rain
And my head, I'd be scratchin' while my thoughts
    were busy hatching—If I only had a brain
I'd unravel ever riddle for any individdle
In trouble or in pain
With the thoughts I'd be thinkin', I could be
    another Lincoln—If I only had a brain
I would not be just a nuffin, my head all full of
    stuffin'
My heart all full of pain
And perhaps I'd deserve you & be even worthy
    erv you—If I only had a brain

When a man's an empty kettle, he should be
    upon his mettle
And yet I'm torn apart
Just because I'm presumin' that I could be
    kinda human—If I only had a heart
I'd be tender, I'd be gentle, & awful sentimental
Regarding love & art
I'd be friends with the sparrows & the boy that
    shoots the arrows—If I only had a heart
Just to register emotion, Jealousy, Devotion
And really feel the part
I would stay young & chipper & I'd lock it with a
    zipper—If I only had a heart

Life is sad believe me missy, when you're born
    to be a sissy—Without the vim & verve
But I could change my habits, never more be
    scared of rabbits—If I only had the nerve
I'm afraid there's no denyin' I'm just a
    dandelion—A fate I don't deserve
But I could show my prowess, be a lion, not a
    mowess—If I only had the nerve
I would show the dinosaurus, who's big around
    the forres'—A king they better serve
Why with my regal beezer I could be another
    Caesar—If I only had the nerve

Red River Valley

From this valley they say you are going,
We will miss your bright eyes & sweet smile
For they say you are taking the sunshine
Which has brightened our pathway a while.

Come and sit by my side if you love me,
Do not hasten to bid me adieu

But remember the Red River Valley
And the one who has loved you so true.

Won't you think of the valley you're leaving,
Oh how lonely, how sad it will be?
Just think of the fond heart you are breaking
And the grief you are causing to me.

As you go to your home by the ocean,
May you never forget those sweet hours
That we spent in the Red River Valley
And the love we exchanged 'mid the flowers.

Riddle Song

I gave my love a cherry that had no stone,
I gave my love a chicken that had no bone,
I gave my love a story that had no end,
I gave my love a baby with no cryin'.

How can there be a cherry that has no stone?
How can there be a chicken that has no bone?
How can there be a story that had no end?
How can there be a baby with no cryin'?

A cherry as it's bloomin' it has no stone,
A chicken when an egg it has no bone,
A story of "I love you" it has no end,
A baby when it's sleepin' has no cryin'.

Goodnight Irene
**(Chorus): Irene goodnight, Irene goodnight
Goodnight Irene, goodnight Irene, I'll see you
    in my dreams**

Sometimes I live in the country, sometimes I live
    in town,
Sometimes I have a great notion, to get out and
    wander around.   **—chorus—**
I love Irene, God knows I do, I'll love her 'til the
    seas run dry
And if Irene turns her back to me, I'll roam the
    mountains high.   **—chorus—**

Foxes sleep in the forest, lions sleep in their dens
Goats sleep on the mountainside & piggies sleep
    in pens.   **—chorus—**
Whales sleep in the ocean, zebras sleep on land,
Hippos sleep by the riverside & camels sleep on
    sand.   **—chorus—**
Coyote sleeps in the canyon, a birdie sleeps in a
    tree,
And when it's time for me to rest, my tent's the
    place for me.   **—chorus—**

If You're Happy & You Know It

If you're happy & you know it clap your hands
If you're happy & you know it clap your hands
If you're happy & you know it, let everybody
show it
If you're happy & you know it, clap your hands

2— stamp your feet 3—slap your knees 4—
do a dance 5— shout hurrah 6— shout hurrah,
do a dance, slap you knees, stamp your feet, if
you're happy and you know it, clap your hands

Sweet Betsy

Did you ever hear tell of Sweet Betsy from Pike,
Who crossed the wide mountains with her lover
Ike,
With two yoke of cattle and one spotted hog,
A tall Shangai rooster and an old yellow dog.

They swam the wide river and climbed the tall
peaks
And camped on the prairies for weeks upon
weeks,
Starvation and illness, hard work and slaughter,
They reached California in spite of high-water.

They passed the Sierras through mountains of
snow,
'Til old California was sighted below.
Sweet Betsy she hollered, and Ike gave a cheer,
Saying, "Betsy, my darlin', I'm a made millioneer."

Long Ike and Sweet Betsy became husband and
wife,
Built up a family and had a grand life.
And Betsy, well satisfied, said with a smile,
"I've got all I need within half a mile."

Clementine

In a cavern, in a canyon, excavating for a mine
Lived a miner, '49-er, & his daughter Clementine

**(Chorus): Oh my darling, Oh my darling, Oh
my darling, Clementine
You are lost and gone forever, dreadful
sorry, Clementine**

Light she was & like a fairy & her shoes were
number 9
Herring boxes without topses, sandals were for
Clementine   —chorus—

She drove the ducklings to the water every
morning just at nine
Stubbed her toe against a splinter, fell into the
foaming brine   —chorus—
Ruby lips above the water, blowing bubbles
soft and fine
But alas! I was no swimmer, so I lost my
Clementine   —chorus—
In a churchyard near the canyon where the
myrtle does entwine
There grow roses, other posies, fertilized by
Clementine   —chorus—
Then the miner, '49-er, soon began to peak &
pine
Thought he oughter join his daughter, now he
with his Clementine   —chorus—
In my dreams she still does haunt me, robed
in garments soaked with brine
Tho' in life I used to hug her, now she's dead,
draw the line   —chorus—
Oh ye campers, heed this warning to this trag
tale of mine
CPR, it would have saved her, Oh my darling
Clementine   —chorus—

Buffalo Gals

Buffalo gals won't you—come out tonight,
come out tonight, come out tonight
Buffalo gals won't you come out tonight &
dance by the light of the moon

As I was walking—*down the street (3x)*
A pretty girl I chanced to meet beneath the
silver moon

I asked her if she'd—*stop & talk (3x)*
Her feet covered up the whole sidewalk, she
was fair to view

I asked her if she'd—*be my wife (3x)*
Then I'd be happy all my life if she'd marry me

Oh I danced with the dolly with a hole in her
stocking
And her feet kept a-rocking & her knees kept
a-knocking
Oh I danced with the dolly with a hole in her
stocking
And we danced by the light of the moon

If I Only Had a Brain

could while away the hours, conferin' with the
   flowers
Consultin' with the rain
And my head, I'd be scratchin' while my thoughts
   were busy hatching—If I only had a brain
d unravel ever riddle for any individdle
n trouble or in pain
With the thoughts I'd be thinkin', I could be
   another Lincoln—If I only had a brain
would not be just a nuffin, my head all full of
   stuffin'
My heart all full of pain
And perhaps I'd deserve you & be even worthy
   erv you—If I only had a brain

When a man's an empty kettle, he should be
   upon his mettle
And yet I'm torn apart
Just because I'm presumin' that I could be
   kinda human—If I only had a heart
'd be tender, I'd be gentle, & awful sentimental
Regarding love & art
'd be friends with the sparrows & the boy that
   shoots the arrows—If I only had a heart
Just to register emotion, Jealousy, Devotion
And really feel the part
would stay young & chipper & I'd lock it with a
   zipper—If I only had a heart

Life is sad believe me missy, when you're born
   to be a sissy—Without the vim & verve
But I could change my habits, never more be
   scared of rabbits—If I only had the nerve
'm afraid there's no denyin' I'm just a
   dandelion—A fate I don't deserve
But I could show my prowess, be a lion, not a
   mowess—If I only had the nerve
would show the dinosaurus, who's big around
   the forres'—A king they better serve
Why with my regal beezer I could be another
   Caesar—If I only had the nerve

Red River Valley

rom this valley they say you are going,
We will miss your bright eyes & sweet smile
or they say you are taking the sunshine
Which has brightened our pathway a while.

ome and sit by my side if you love me,
o not hasten to bid me adieu

But remember the Red River Valley
And the one who has loved you so true.

Won't you think of the valley you're leaving,
Oh how lonely, how sad it will be?
Just think of the fond heart you are breaking
And the grief you are causing to me.

As you go to your home by the ocean,
May you never forget those sweet hours
That we spent in the Red River Valley
And the love we exchanged 'mid the flowers.

Riddle Song

I gave my love a cherry that had no stone,
I gave my love a chicken that had no bone,
I gave my love a story that had no end,
I gave my love a baby with no cryin'.

How can there be a cherry that has no stone?
How can there be a chicken that has no bone?
How can there be a story that had no end?
How can there be a baby with no cryin'?

A cherry as it's bloomin' it has no stone,
A chicken when an egg it has no bone,
A story of "I love you" it has no end,
A baby when it's sleepin' has no cryin'.

Goodnight Irene
**(Chorus): Irene goodnight, Irene goodnight
Goodnight Irene, goodnight Irene, I'll see you
   in my dreams**

Sometimes I live in the country, sometimes I live
   in town,
Sometimes I have a great notion, to get out and
   wander around.   —chorus—
I love Irene, God knows I do, I'll love her 'til the
   seas run dry
And if Irene turns her back to me, I'll roam the
   mountains high.   —chorus—

Foxes sleep in the forest, lions sleep in their dens
Goats sleep on the mountainside & piggies sleep
   in pens.   —chorus—
Whales sleep in the ocean, zebras sleep on land,
Hippos sleep by the riverside & camels sleep on
   sand.   —chorus—
Coyote sleeps in the canyon, a birdie sleeps in a
   tree,
And when it's time for me to rest, my tent's the
   place for me.   —chorus—

SONG SHEET—REMOVE AND CUT

If You're Happy & You Know It
If you're happy & you know it clap your hands
If you're happy & you know it clap your hands
If you're happy & you know it, let everybody
show it
If you're happy & you know it, clap your hands

2— stamp your feet   3—slap your knees   4—
do a dance   5— shout hurrah   6— shout hurrah,
do a dance, slap you knees, stamp your feet, if
you're happy and you know it, clap your hands

Sweet Betsy
Did you ever hear tell of Sweet Betsy from Pike,
Who crossed the wide mountains with her lover
Ike,
With two yoke of cattle and one spotted hog,
A tall Shangai rooster and an old yellow dog.

They swam the wide river and climbed the tall
peaks
And camped on the prairies for weeks upon
weeks,
Starvation and illness, hard work and slaughter,
They reached California in spite of high-water.

They passed the Sierras through mountains of
snow,
'Til old California was sighted below.
Sweet Betsy she hollered, and Ike gave a cheer,
Saying, "Betsy, my darlin', I'm a made millioneer."

Long Ike and Sweet Betsy became husband and
wife,
Built up a family and had a grand life.
And Betsy, well satisfied, said with a smile,
"I've got all I need within half a mile."

Clementine
In a cavern, in a canyon, excavating for a mine
Lived a miner, '49-er, & his daughter Clementine

**(Chorus): Oh my darling, Oh my darling, Oh
my darling, Clementine
You are lost and gone forever, dreadful
sorry, Clementine**

Light she was & like a fairy & her shoes were
number 9
Herring boxes without topses, sandals were for
Clementine   —chorus—

She drove the ducklings to the water every
morning just at nine
Stubbed her toe against a splinter, fell into the
foaming brine   —chorus—
Ruby lips above the water, blowing bubbles
soft and fine
But alas! I was no swimmer, so I lost my
Clementine   —chorus—
In a churchyard near the canyon where the
myrtle does entwine
There grow roses, other posies, fertilized by
Clementine   —chorus—
Then the miner, '49-er, soon began to peak &
pine
Thought he oughter join his daughter, now he
with his Clementine   —chorus—
In my dreams she still does haunt me, robed
in garments soaked with brine
Tho' in life I used to hug her, now she's dead,
draw the line   —chorus—
Oh ye campers, heed this warning to this trag
tale of mine
CPR, it would have saved her, Oh my darling
Clementine   —chorus—

Buffalo Gals
Buffalo gals won't you—come out tonight,
come out tonight, come out tonight
Buffalo gals won't you come out tonight &
dance by the light of the moon

As I was walking—*down the street (3x)*
A pretty girl I chanced to meet beneath the
silver moon

I asked her if she'd—*stop & talk (3x)*
Her feet covered up the whole sidewalk, she
was fair to view

I asked her if she'd—*be my wife (3x)*
Then I'd be happy all my life if she'd marry me

Oh I danced with the dolly with a hole in her
stocking
And her feet kept a-rocking & her knees kept
a-knocking
Oh I danced with the dolly with a hole in her
stocking
And we danced by the light of the moon

Song Sheet—Remove and Cut

And another thing—I've noticed a good deal—and there's no bird, or cow, or anything that uses as good grammar as a bluejay. You may say a cat uses good grammar. Well, a cat does—but you let a cat get excited once; you let a cat get to pulling fur with another cat on a shed and you'll hear grammar that will give you the lockjaw.

Ignorant people think it's the *noise* which fighting cats make that is so aggravating, but it ain't so; it's the sickening grammar they use. Now, I've never heard a jay use bad grammar but very seldom; and when they do, they are as ashamed as a human; they shut right down and leave.

Now, on top of all this, there's another thing; a jay can out-swear any gentleman in the mines. You think a cat can swear. Well, a cat can—but you give a bluejay a subject that calls for his reserve-powers, and where is your cat? Don't talk to *me*—I know too much about this thing.

And there's yet another thing; in the one little particular of scolding—just good, clean, out-and-out scolding—a bluejay can lay over anything, human or divine. Yes, sir, a jay is everything that a man is.

A jay can cry, a jay can laugh, a jay can feel shame, a jay can reason and plan and discuss, a jay likes gossip and scandal, a jay has got a sense of humor, a jay knows when he is an ass just as well as you do—maybe better. If a jay ain't human, he better take in his sign, that's all there is to it.

Now I'm going to tell you a perfectly true fact about some bluejays. When I first begun to understand jay language correctly, there was a little incident happened here.

29

Seven years ago, the last man in this region but me moved away. There stands his house—been empty ever since; a log house, with a plank roof—just one big room, and no more; no ceiling—nothing between the rafters and the floor. Well, one Sunday morning I was sitting out

here in front of my cabin, with my cat, taking the sun, and looking at the blue hills, and listening to the leaves rustling so lonely in the trees, and thinking of the home away yonder in the states, that I hadn't heard from in thirteen years, when a bluejay lit on that house, with an acorn in his mouth, and says, "Hello, I reckon I've struck something."

When he spoke, the acorn dropped out of his mouth and rolled down the roof, of course, but he didn't care; his mind was all on the thing he had struck. It was a knot-hole in the roof. He cocked his head to one side, shut one eye and put the other one to the hole, like a possum looking down a jug; then he glanced up with his bright eyes, gave a wink or two with his wings—which signifies gratification, you understand—and says, "It looks like a hole, it's located like a hole—blamed if I don't believe it *is* a hole!"

Then he cocked his head down and took another look; he glances up, perfectly joyful, this time; winks his wings and tail both, and says, "Oh no, this ain't no fat thing, I reckon! If I ain't in luck!—why it's a perfectly elegant hole!" So he flew down and got that acorn, and fetched it up and dropped it in, and was just tilting his

30

head back, with the heavenliest smile on his face, when all of a sudden he was paralyzed into a listening attitude and that smile faded gradually out of his countenance like breath off'n a razor, and the queerest look of surprise took its place. Then he says, "Why, I didn't hear it fall!" He cocked his eye at the hole again, and took a long look; raised up and shook his head; stepped around to the other side of the hole and took another look from that side; shook his head again.

He studied a while, then he just went into the *details*—walked round and round the hole and spied into it from every point of the compass. No use. Now he took a thinking attitude on the comb of the roof and scratched the back of his head with his right foot a minute, and finally says, "Well, it's too many for *me*, that's certain; must be a mighty long hole; however, I ain't got no time to fool around here, I got to 'tend to business, I reckon it's all right—I'll chance it, anyway."

So he flew off and fetched another acorn and dropped it in, and tried to flirt his eye to the hole quick enough to see what become of it, but he was too late. He held his eye there as much as a minute; then he raised up and sighed, and says, "Confound it, I don't seem to understand this thing, no way; however, I'll tackle her again." He fetched another acorn, and done his level best to see what become of it, but he couldn't.

He says, "Well, *I* never struck no such hole as this before; I'm of the opinion it's a totally new kind of hole." Then he begun to get mad. He held in for a spell, walking up and down the comb of the roof and shaking his head and muttering to himself; but his feelings got the upper hand of

31

him presently, and he broke loose and cussed himself black in the face. I never see a bird take on so about a little thing.

When he got through he walks to the hole and looks in again for half a minute; then he says, "Well, you're a long hole and a deep hole and a mighty singular hole altogether—but I've started in to fill you, and I'm cursed if I *don't* fill you, if it takes a hundred years!"

And with that, away he went. You never see a bird work so since you was born. He laid into his work, and the way he hove acorns into that hole for about two hours and a half was one of the most exciting and astonishing spectacles I ever struck. He never stopped to take a look any more—he just hove 'em in and went for more.

Well, at last he could hardly flop his wings, he was so tuckered out. He comes a-drooping down, once more, sweating like an ice-pitcher, drops his acorn in and says, "*Now* I guess I've got the bulge on you by this time!" So he bent down for a look. If you'll believe me, when his head come up again he was just pale with rage.

He says, "I've shoveled acorns enough in there to keep the family thirty years, and if I can see a sign of one of 'em I wish I may land in a museum with a belly full of sawdust in two minutes!"

He just had strength enough to crawl up onto the comb and lean his back agin' the chimbly, and then he collected his impressions and begun to free his mind. I see in a second that what I had mistook for profanity in the mines was only just the rudiments, as you may say.

Another jay was going by, and heard him doing his devotions, and stops to inquire what was up. The sufferer told him the whole circumstance, and says, "How many did you say you put in there?" "Not any less than two tons," says the sufferer. The other jay went and looked

32

again. He couldn't seem to make it out, so he raised a yell, and three more jays come. They all examined the hole, they all made the sufferer tell it over again, then they all discussed it and got off as many leather-headed opinions about it as an crowd of humans could have done.

They called in more jays; then more and more, 'til pretty soon this whole region 'peared to have a blue flush about it. There must have been five thousand of them; and such another jawing and disputing and ripping and cussing, you never heard.

Every jay in the whole lot put his eye to the hole and delivered a more chuckle-headed opinion about the mystery than the jay that went there before him. They examined the house all over, too. The door was standing half open and at last one old jay happened to go and light on it and look in.

Of course, that knocked the mystery galley-west in a second. There lay the acorns, scattered all over the floor. He flopped his wings and raised a whoop. "Come here!" he says, "Come here, everybody; hang'd if this fool hasn't been trying to fill up a house with acorns!"

They all came a-swooping down like a blue cloud and as each fellow lit on the door and took a glance, the whole absurdity of the contract that first jay had tackled hit him home and he fell over backward suffocating with laughter and the next jay took his place and done the same.

Well, sir, they roosted around here on the housetop and the trees for an hour and guffawed over that thing like human beings. It ain't any use to tell me a bluejay hasn't got a sense of humor, because I know better. And memory, too.

They brought jays here from all over the United States to look down that hole, every summer for three years. Other birds, too. And they could all see the point, except an owl that come from Nova Scotia to visit the Yo Semite and he took this thing in on his way back. He said he couldn't see anything funny in it. But then he was a good deal disappointed about Yo Semite, too.
—Mark Twain, from *A Tramp Abroad*

 ## Buffalo Gals

A
Buffalo gals won't you come out tonight,
   E   A
   come out tonight, come out tonight
A
Buffalo gals won't you come out tonight &
   E   A
   dance by the light of the moon

A   E
As I was walking down the street, down the street,
   A
   down the street,
A   E   A
A pretty girl I chanced to meet beneath the silver moon
——Chorus——
I asked her if she'd— *stop & talk (3x)*
Her feet took up the whole sidewalk, she was fair to view
——Chorus——
I asked her if she'd— *be my wife (3x)*
I'd be happy all my life, if she'd marry me
——Chorus——
Oh, I danced with the dolly with a hole in her stocking
And her feet kept a-rocking & her knees kept a-knocking
Oh, I danced with the dolly with a hole in her stocking
And we danced by the light of the moon

If I Only Had a Brain

D   G

I could while away the hours, conferin' with the flowers

D

Consultin' with the rain

            G   A7

And my head, I'd be scratchin' while my thoughts were

                              G   D

busy hatching—If I only had a brain

I'd unravel every riddle for any individdle
In trouble or in pain
With the thoughts I'd be thinkin', I could be another
      Lincoln—If I only had a brain
I would not be just a nuffin, my head all full of stuffin'
My heart all full of pain
And perhaps I'd deserve you & be even worthy erv
      you—If I only had a brain

When a man's an empty kettle he should be upon his
      mettle
And yet I'm torn apart
Just because I'm presumin' that I could be kinda
      human—If I only had a heart
I'd be tender I'd be gentle, & awful sentimental
Regarding love & art
I'd be friends with the sparrows & the boy that shoots
      the arrows—If I only had a heart
Just to register Emotion, Jealousy, Devotion
And really feel the part
I would stay young & chipper & I'd lock it with a zipper
      —If I only had a heart

Life is sad believe me missy, when you're born to be a
      sissy—Without the vim & verve
But I could change my habits, never more be scared of
      rabbits—If I only had the nerve
I'm afraid there's no denyin' I'm just a dandelion
A fate I don't deserve

But I could show my prowess, be a lion, not a mowess
   —If I only had the nerve
I would show the dinosaurus, who's big around the forres'
   —A king they better serve
Why with my regal beezer I could be another Caesar
   —If I only had the nerve

Got to Get Away

Ask around the campfire for a
word to put in each blank—when
complete, give it someone to read aloud.

*(Name of Female Camper)*_____decided
she couldn't stand another day as a *(job)* _____
and needed to take herself and her *(pet)* _____
to the mountains for *(number)* _____ days.

So she stuffed her *(thing)* _____, her *(thing)* _____
and some extra *(things)* _____ into her
(container) _____. She kissed her *(thing)* _____
good-bye, locked the *(thing)* _____ and hopped into
her *(type of transportation)* _____.

In *(number)* _____ *(unit of time)* _____, she
got to the trailhead at *(a place in the Sierra Nevadas)*
_____. When she arrived, she took off
her *(article of clothing)* _____ and slipped
into her *(clothing)* _____.

As she started climbing towards *(thing)* _____
Lake, she whistled the refrain from *(name of song)*

_____.

A band of (wild animal) _____s heard all the racket and stuck out their (body part) _____s to investigate. When they saw this (adjective) _____ woman, wearing a (color) _____ (type of clothing) _____, a (color)_____ (type of clothing) _____ and a (color) _____ (type of clothing)_____ carrying (an object) _____ and a (musical instrument) _____. It scared the (thing) _____ out of them and they (type of movement) _____ away as fast as they could.

When night fell, she got cold and started to (verb) _____ up and down to keep warm. Pretty soon she got hungry and cooked up a big batch of (food) _____ and (another food) _____ and washed it down with (number) _____ glasses of (liquid)_____.

She became sleepy and (verb) _____ed into her sleeping bag. She tossed and turned and (verb) _____ed all night and when she (verb) _____ed up in the morning realized she had been sleeping right smack dab in a patch of (plant) _____, which caused her to itch and break out in (2 colors) _____ and _____ spots all over her (body part) _____.

The next morning, she went to see a (profession) _____. She was told this was an extremely bad case of (disease) _____ and sent her straight to (place) _____. Boy, I never thought camping would be this (adjective)_____.
I should do this about once every (measurement of time)_____.

One-Eye Bennett Goes Hunting

Did I ever tell you about the time One-Eyed Bennett went hunting?

He and his family lived up near the middle fork of the San Joaquin and had a snug cabin, a dandy spring of good water just outside the door and plenty of wood cut and stacked. But times were hard and he hadn't had much luck earning cash that summer. Old Bennett, his bespectacled wife, Four-Eyes, and their six daughters and one son—Amy, Kate, Molly, Maddy, Annie, Grace and Carlos (who all had two eyes) were mighty hungry and winter was looming on the horizon. So One-Eye hitched his horse, Three-Eyes, to a wagon and headed out to Graveyard Meadows to see what he could scare up.

After he had gone a piece he saw a pair of red squirrels sitting in a pine tree. He loaded one of his precious shells in the chamber of his rifle and decided to try and line them up just right, so he could kill both with one bullet. One-Eye must have snuck around a half hour, trying to get a bead on the squirrels.

Whenever he got close, they'd scamper around and he'd lose his chance.

Finally patience paid off, not only did he get both critters in his sights, but a big old gray squirrel that was coming over to steal pine nuts got in the line of fire. Old One-Eye pulled the trigger and shot all three.

Just then he heard a bunch of wild turkeys start squawking to beat the band. He looked over and saw eight hens and two toms flapping their wings and wiggling about, but they were stuck in place. It seemed after that bullet went through all three squirrels it ricocheted off a stone and hit the branch of an old oak tree the gobblers were sitting on, splitting the limb and catching those turkeys' legs in the crack, like a clothespin.

Bennett climbed up the tree and got the turkeys before they busted loose. But, as he started back down, he lost his footing and fell out, landing hard in a big old pile of brush. He had to scramble and fight his way out of the sticks, weeds, and vines. Before he freed himself, One-Eye had smothered a covey of quails and two big rabbits with his thrashing.

He tied up the turkeys, quail and rabbits and went back to get his squirrels. One had fallen into the creek, so he waded in to snag him. But the water was deeper than

Bennett had figured and when he came back up, sputtering, with the squirrel in his hand, he found his pockets, boot tops and shirt neck were full of fish—mostly brook trout, but with a few rainbows thrown in. There was also a pair of turtles, one up each pant leg.

As he was stringing the fish, he reached around to slap a mosquito biting the back of his neck and one of the buttons on his shirt popped off and went zinging into a redbud thicket. He marked the spot to go get it when he was done, but he soon heard an awful gasping and hacking sound coming from the redbuds.

One-Eye dropped his fish and snuck over to check what the commotion was. As he poked his head in, he saw a big buck deer rolling on the ground, kicking and jerking, just getting ready to die. Bennett was scared because he didn't know what had killed the critter, but he screwed himself up and cut the deer's throat to end his misery and bleed him to death. As he opened the deer, he saw his button stuck in the deer's windpipe! That buck must have opened his mouth to belch just as that button came flying through and it went down his throat and cut off his air supply.

As One-Eye was throwing a rope over a branch to

hoist that deer so he could skin it out, he noticed a bunch of bees going in and out of a hole way up in an old black walnut tree. He climbed a good 60 feet to get at that honey, stuffing his pockets full of nuts while he shinnied up.

When he reached the hive he slowly and carefully put his hand in the hollow

40

among the bees, reaching to pull out pieces of honeycomb. Bennett would shake the bees off and put the comb inside of his hat. He reached further and further, 'til his arm was in as far as it would go and his feet were dangling off the limb he had stood on.

Bennett hadn't been eating too much lately, and was pretty skinny. As he hung there, the weight of those walnuts pulled his britches off. One-Eye hung by his arm, in his underwear, as his pants fluttered to the ground. An angry bee flew in the trap door of his long johns and stung him down in the nether regions. One-Eye jolted upward with the hot flash of pain and, as he was falling, he saw his pants land on a black bear just crawling out of her den near the base of the tree. Blinded and angry from having a pair of trousers covering her head, the bear plunged full speed ahead, growling and howling like there was no tomorrow. She ran smack dab square into a large granite boulder, stunning herself and collapsing on the ground, dazed and stupefied.

As he continued falling, Bennett saw a V of fat geese flying low towards a backwater spot in the creek. He reached out and grabbed one by the neck right before he hit the bear, who let out a big whoosh of air, which both softened One-Eye's landing and knocked the wind out of her.

Bennett made quick work of killing and skinning that bear and loaded the bounty in the wagon. Let me tell you, those kids were awful glad to see 3 squirrels, 10 turkeys, 41 quail, 2 rabbits, 35 pounds of trout, a couple of turtles, a 12 point buck, a pail full of black walnuts, 16 pieces of honeycomb, a fat goose, and 220 pounds of bear meat rolling home, all brought down with a single shot.

Red River Valley

E
From this valley they say you are going

B 7
We will miss your bright eyes & sweet smile

E   E 7   A
For they say you are taking the sunshine

B 7   E
Which has brightened our pathway a while

Come and sit by my side if you love me
Do not hasten to bid me adieu
But remember the Red River Valley
And the one who has loved you so true

Won't you think of the valley you're leaving
Oh how lonely, how sad it will be?
Just think of the fond heart you're breaking
And the grief you are causing to me

As you go to your home by the ocean
May you never forget those sweet hours
That we spent in the Red River Valley
And the love we exchanged 'mid the flowers

A COTILLION PARTY OF THIRTY-TWO PERSONS DANCING ON THE STUMP OF THE MAMMOTH TREE.

RIDDLE SONG

E   A   E
I gave my love a cherry that had no stone
B 7   E   B 7
I gave my love a chicken that had no bone
B 7   E   B 7
I gave my love a story that had no end
E   A   E
I gave my love a baby with no cryin'

How can there be a cherry that has no stone?
How can there be a chicken that has no bone?
How can there be a story that had no end?
How can there be a baby with no cryin?

A cherry as it's bloomin' it has no stone
A chicken when an egg it has no bone
A story of "I love you" it has no end
A baby when it's sleepin' has no cryin'

BEAR BELLS

Way back when—a few years after white settlers first started visiting the Sierra, a city dweller decided to go on a hike up the Kaweah River, through what is now part of King's Canyon National Park. Just before he left the last out-post, the dude stopped in a small general store to pick up supplies. A withered old man sat outside on a boulder in the sun. As the tenderfoot approached, the old man slowly rose and hobbled behind the counter inside his store.

After selecting some gear and camp food, the stranger started to chat with the storeowner, who had lived

43

so long in the sun and wind and weather that his face was like the mountains—full of ridges and valleys.

"Howdy, old timer, I'm going hiking in this area and was wondering if there are any bears around here?"

"Yup," replied the owner.

"What kind?" asked the hiker nervously.

"Well, we got both kinds, black bears and grizzlies," he answered.

"I see," said the hiker, feeling his palms get warm and damp and the sweat start to trickle down his armpits. "Do you have any of those bear bells?"

"What do you mean?" questioned the old timer.

"You know, the little tinkle bells for folks to wear in bear country," said the city fella. "So the bears can hear you coming and you don't surprise them and get attacked."

"Yup, we got those over there," said the storeowner, directing the dude to a shelf on the other side of the store.

The hiker shook every one of the entire shelf of bells, picked out a couple and took them back to the counter to pay. "Say mister," he inquired, "how can you tell when you're in bear territory, anyway?"

"By the scat. You know, the droppings" said the owner.

"Well how can you tell the difference between grizzly scat and black bear scat?" asked the hiker, starting to get nervous again.

"By what's in it," answered the owner.

The city fella was starting to get frustrated. "So what's in grizzly scat that isn't in black bear scat?" he asked.

"Bear bells," replied the old man, handing the hiker his purchases.

In the Midst of the Yosemite Fall

John Muir considered the falls of the Sierra one of the most sublime of pleasures. He was particularly captivated by the rainbows the falling sprays made when lit in just the right way by the sun.

Muir roamed the falls at night, finding the odd mixture of thrills, humbleness and peace he sought under the moon's light. In the following selection, he describes his harrowing experience in viewing a lunar rainbow from behind Yosemite Fall.

"...toward midnight, after spending a few hours with the wild beauty of the Upper Fall, I sauntered along the edge of the gorge, looking in here and there, wherever the footing felt safe, to see what I could learn of the night aspects of the smaller falls that dwell there.

Down in an exceedingly black, pit-like portion of the gorge, at the foot of the highest of the intermediate falls, into which the moonbeams were pouring through a narrow opening, I saw a well-defined spray-bow, beautifully distinct in colors, spanning the pit from side to side, while pure white foam-waves beneath the beautiful bow were constantly springing up out of the dark into the moonlight like dancing ghosts.

A wild scene, but not a safe one, is made by the moon as it appears through the edge of the Yosemite Fall when one is behind it. Once, after enjoying the night-song

45

of the waters and watching the formation of the colored bow as the moon came 'round the domes and sent her beams into the wild uproar, I ventured out on the narrow bench that extends back of the fall from Fern Ledge and began to admire the dim-veiled grandeur of the view.

I could see the fine gauzy threads of the fall's filmy border by having the light in front; and wishing to look at the moon through the meshes of some of the denser portions of the falls, I ventured to creep farther behind while it was gently wind-swayed. I had not given sufficient thought about the consequences of its swaying back to its natural position after the wind-pressure should be removed.

The effect was enchanting: fine, savage music sounding above, beneath, around me; while the moon, apparently in the very midst of the rushing waters, seemed to be struggling to keep her place, on account of the ever-varying form and density of the water masses through which she was seen, now darkly veiled or eclipsed by a rush of thick-headed comets, now flashing out through openings between their tails.

I was in fairyland between the dark wall and the wild throng of illumined waters, but suffered sudden disenchantment; for in an instant all was dark. Down came a dash of spent comets, thin and harmless-looking in the distance, but they felt desperately solid and stony when they struck my shoulders, like a mixture of choking spray and gravel and big hail-stones.

Instinctively dropping on my knees, I gripped an angle of the rock, curled up like a young fern frond with my face pressed against my breast, and in this attitude submitted as best I could to my thundering bath. The heavier masses seemed to strike like cobblestones, and there was a confused noise of many waters about my ears—hissing, gurgling, clashing sounds that were not heard as music.

46

The situation was quickly realized. How fast one's thoughts burn in such times of stress! I was weighing chance of my escape. Would the column be swayed a few inches away from the wall, or would it come yet closer? The fall was in flood and not so lightly would its ponderous mass be swayed. My fate seemed to depend on a breath of the "idle wind." It was moved gently forward, the pounding ceased, and I was once more visited by glimpses of the moon.

But fearing I might be caught at a disadvantage in making too hasty a retreat, I moved only a few feet along the bench to where a block of ice lay. I wedged myself between the ice and the wall, and lay face downwards, until the steadiness of the light gave encouragement to rise and get away.

Somewhat nerve-shaken, drenched, and benumbed, I made out to build a fire, warmed myself, ran home, reached my cabin before daylight, got an hour or two of sleep, and awoke sound and comfortable, better, not worse, for my hard midnight bath.

—John Muir *(slightly abridged)*

The Onion Eaters

Long ago and high in the Sierra, along the Kings River, Western Mono Native Americans spent the fair months hunting, fishing, gathering foods and living the life of their tribal custom. They became skilled at managing nature's gifts, harvesting only what was needed to provide food, shelter, warmth and everyday necessities. They were happy and as familiar with magic and the spirit realm as they were with the material world.

Among these people lived six women, skilled gatherers, accomplished and highly regarded by their people. Each was married to a man of their tribe, and those six men were hunters of the mountain lion.

On a day when the sun was gold, the sky was blue and large white clouds flew above them, the wives were on the mountainside, picking tender clover greens for the evening meal. One of them came upon a new plant in an area where the ground was moist and springy. She took a nibble and found the taste wonderful. They were wild onions.

Her friends tasted them and all found them delicious. The six Mono women continued to eat until they were full, then gathered some for their husbands and went home to prepare the evening meal.

As the mountains glowed in the evening just before dark, the husbands came home, tired but happy. Each had killed a big mountain lion.

"Phew! What is that awful smell?" asked the

husbands of the women. As they came closer they realized the odor came from the breath of their wives!

"We have found a new plant that grows in abundance," said the woman who first found them. "Here, taste. They are delicious."

The husbands refused to even taste the onions. They found the smell horrible and made their wives sleep outside that evening. The women were unhappy. They wanted to be with their men and didn't like spending the night alone in the chill air.

In the morning the men went hunting again. The wives went back to the onion patch and couldn't restrain themselves from eating more, they found the taste so delicious.

When the husbands returned that evening, none of them had been successful in the hunt. They were upset. "The lions could smell that odor on us," said one of the men. "We failed to even see one, they would run away."

When the men again detected onions on the women's breath, they became angry and again made them sleep outside.

This continued for six days. Every evening the men came home exhausted, unsuccessful in their hunt. Each night they smelled the onions their wives had eaten that day and raged. "Go away!" they commanded. "Leave us!" We can't hunt, the smell keeps us awake all night. We are unhappy. We don't want you anymore. Go away!"

The women were despondent. The next morning they went together to the onion patch. Each carried with her a magic rope woven from the finest and lightest down of the eagle.

"Our husbands no longer love us," said one of the

wives. "Let's leave them forever." The others agreed. They climbed up a steep rock, each carrying her eagle-down rope. At the very top they rested.

"Do you still want to leave your husbands forever?" asked one.

"Yes!" they all answered. So they spoke a magic Mono word and the woman who found the onions threw her eagle-down rope straight up. It lengthened as it uncurled, the middle of the line catching on a piece of the blue Sierra sky. Both ends hung back down to the ground.

The others tied their own ropes to the ends and joined hands in a circle. "Eagle-down ropes, magic ropes, help us leave our husbands, who no longer love and respect us."

They started to sing a special Mono magic song. Because their life was full of spirit and belief, and because

they had magic eagle-down ropes, the ropes slowly started to rise and the ends began swinging in ever-widening circles.

The wives sang louder and rose higher in the sky. Soon they were sailing through the blue Sierra sky over their village, joined in a circle at the base of their magic eagle-down ropes.

Their fathers and mothers, sisters and brothers, friends and relations all looked up and saw them swinging in the sky. The people ran to their huts and brought out offerings of precious things—acorn mush and baskets and fine cloths made from the skins of animals.

"Come back!" the Mono people cried. "See what we give you?" But the women continued to circle higher in the blue Sierra sky on their magic eagle-down ropes.

Their husbands looked up and saw them.

"Why didn't you keep an eye on them?" scolded the women's parents. "Why did you treat them badly and make them go away?"

The men felt miserable. They realized they were wrong and grew lonesome and sad. They met and thought of what to do. It was decided they would use their own magic eagle-down ropes and go up in the sky after their wives. They climbed the same steep rock and spoke the same magic word and sang the same magic song the same way their wives had done. Soon they too were sailing in the sky over the village.

The people came out again and begged them to come back. But the men wanted their wives so they sang louder and flew higher into the blue Sierra sky.

The women looked down and saw their husbands flying up after them. "Shall we let them catch us and return to the village?" they asked each other.

"No!" said the one who found the onions. "They said they did not want us anymore. We will not return to them, ever." The women agreed. They would rather be alone together in the sky.

When the men got close the women shouted down to them. "Come no further, stay where you are!" Their song and magic was more powerful than their husbands, so the men could go no further, stuck just below their wives high in the sky.

Over time, they all turned into stars and each night you can see them. The higher group is called "The Young Women" by the Monos. It is known as the "Pleiades" by whites, a circle of six stars. The lower set of six stars is called The "Young Men" by the native peoples. Among whites, it has been named "Taurus."

Whatever they are called, they appear every evening, swinging through the Sierra sky, the women shimmering just beyond their husbands' reach, all taken there on the backs of their songs and magic.

✴   ✴   ✴   ✴   ✴   ✴

The Range of Light

...Looking eastward from the summit to the Pacheco Pass one shining morning, a landscape was displayed that after all my wanderings still appears as the most beautiful I have ever beheld.

At my feet lay the Great Central Valley of California, level and flowery, like a lake of pure sunshine—forty or fifty miles wide, five hundred miles long—one rich furred garden of yellow *Compositae.* And from the eastern boundary of this vast golden flower-bed rose the mighty Sierra, miles in height, and so gloriously colored and so radiant it seemed not clothed with light but wholly composed of it, like the wall of some celestial city.

Along the top and extending a good way down was a rich pearl-gray belt of snow; below it a belt of blue and dark purple marking the extension of the forests; and stretching along the base of the range a broad belt of rose-purple; all these colors, from the blue sky to the yellow valley smoothly blending as they do in a rainbow, making a wall of light ineffably fine.

Then it seemed to me that the Sierra should be called, not the Nevada or Snowy Range, but the Range of Light. And after ten years of wandering and wondering in the heart of it, rejoicing in its glorious floods of light, the white beams of the morning streaming through the passes, the noonday radiance on the crystal rocks, the flush of the alpenglow, and the irised spray of countless waterfalls, it still seems above all others the Range of Light.

—John Muir, around 1868, from *The Yosemite*

52

Tomorrow

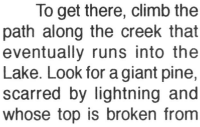

To get there, climb the path along the creek that eventually runs into the Lake. Look for a giant pine, scarred by lightning and whose top is broken from the winds. You'll know it's the right spot if you hear the wind singing through the canopies of the trees.

Watch for a great meadow, a flat, open space with grasses and bush and wildflowers. At the upper end, there is a big fallen log, starting to rot. Hop over and start to go back into the very edge of the forest.

You'll see it—a dark cave formed where two huge slabs of granite are leaning together. Since time began, the ancient hunters and gatherers would use this very place when a sudden afternoon thunderstorm crashed across the mountains. If you sit inside quietly you can feel the lingering spirits of the native peoples.

Can you hear them singing their special songs and chants? Can you sense their presence among these mountain rocks and trees? Their feet traveled over the same ground you are hiking, the paths you walk are the same paths they took.

If you go to the end of the cave, you'll see another entrance, smaller than the one you first went through. Go ahead, squeeze through. If you have chosen the right trail, and thought the right thoughts, you might come out into another, more secret, meadow. It is only accessible to boys and girls who have the adventure to explore.

Pick a shady place to sit down. Maybe over there, next to the granite slab where a spring trickles down. The rock's face is covered with moss and ferns and poplar trees sprout along its base, spinning their leaves in the breeze. Can you hear them rustle and rattle all around you?

This meadow is a special place. The people living in the Sierra would travel here to wait for their animal brothers and sisters. No game was ever hunted or killed in this spot.

After putting their minds in order and calming their spirit, the children of the tribes would sit for hours, watching the circle of life unfold around them. There was a whole world in seeing the smallest ant pushing an enormous load up a steep rock, back to its village. Or in the long arching flight of a hawk swooping high in the sky over the meadow, its shadow scattering mice, rabbits and songbirds. Or in the careful, cautious, alert emergence of a family of deer, coming from the woods to feed on the tender shoots of the grassland.

In this spot, if their thoughts were pure, children would be visited by a special animal, one who would choose them and make itself visible. Often that particular animal would give something of itself to the child. A rabbit might convey speed, a Western meadowlark bestow a lovely singing voice, a badger—courage, a butterfly—the skills of adornment in a most beautiful fashion. To each child a unique gift would be given that would set them apart from their sisters and brothers, friends and cousins. It would become one of their special skills.

The times haven't changed. If you are willing to explore and sit among wildlife with a still heart, you will be visited by your animal of special kinship. The one who makes itself known to you will present you with a quality of distinction you can carry for the rest of your life.

IRENE GOODNIGHT

C   G   C
Irene goodnight, Irene goodnight

          C 7   F   G   C
Goodnight Irene goodnight Irene, I'll see you in my dreams

C   G   C
Sometimes I live in the country, sometimes I live in town

                      F   G   C
Sometimes I have a great notion, to get out and wander around
Repeat chorus
I love Irene, God knows I do, I'll love her 'til the seas run dry
And if Irene turns her back to me, I'll roam the mountains high
Repeat chorus
Foxes sleep in the forest, lions sleep in their dens
Goats sleep on the mountainside & piggies sleep in pens
Repeat chorus
Whales sleep in the ocean, zebras sleep on land
Hippos sleep by the riverside & camels sleep on sand
Repeat chorus
Coyote sleeps in the canyon, a birdie sleeps in a tree
And when it's time for me to rest, my tent's the place for me
Repeat chorus

ACKNOWLEDGMENTS

Writing, editing and publishing a book, even one as modest in nature as this, required more skill, time and energy than I possess. So a big thanks goes to everyone at the Santa Cruz Museum of Natural History, the girls of La Selva, The Cehrs-Chiarito family, Paul Rangell & Emily Abbink, Laura French and her dad Tom, John Anderson, and Beth Baugh and our daughter Amy, for their support.

A very special debt of gratitude is owed to Pat Smith for her patience, flexibility and persistence through the countless hours of turning these words and images into book form. She is a true PageMaker.

If you, good reader, know any camp yarns, skits, songs or such you would like to share, please send them to us.

Deep River Jim

Deep River Jim

Yosemite Association
P.O. Box 545
Yosemite, California, 95389
209-379-2648